INVENTIONS
&
GREAT IDEAS

INVENTIONS
&
GREAT
IDEAS

DOROTHEA DEPRISCO

Interior Illustrations
by Robert Roper

SCHOLASTIC INC.
New York Toronto London Auckland Sydney
Mexico City New Delhi Hong Kong

ISBN 0-439-20213-2

12 11 10 9 8 7 6 5 4 3 2 1   1 2 3 4 5 6/0

Printed in the U.S.A.   01

First Scholastic printing, February 2001

TABLE OF CONTENTS

There are so many inventions that we use every day, and yet we probably never think about why or when they were created. In this book you will learn all about the everyday inventions we use and even about some wacky inventions that you'll probably never see!

You may notice that certain inventions have more than one inventor. Sometimes, a particular history book will give credit to one person for an invention and another book will list someone completely different. The fact is, it sometimes takes many people's efforts and many years to create something that truly works.

Don't stop with the inventions in this book! When you're finished reading — look around you. The desk you're sitting at — who invented that? The eraser you're using or the chalkboard in front of you — what are the stories behind those? There is a world of interesting inventions out there, and *you* could be coming up with ideas for the next one!

- Sometimes awesome things are invented and we don't know who did it! For instance, we know the wheel was created sometime between 3200 and 3500 B.C.E. Thanks to this person we now have bicycles, cars, trains, buses, in-line skates, shopping carts, and much more!

- Over 5,000 years ago in Egypt, people began to come up with recipes for toothpaste. We don't know who started it, but we do know that the first toothpaste had ground eggshells in it. What did the ancient Egyptians use for toothbrushes? Why, their fingers of course!

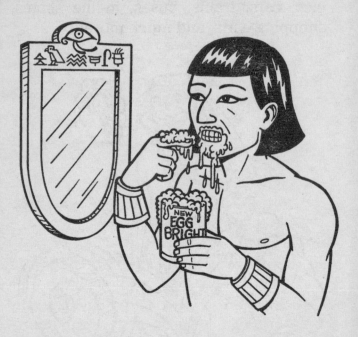

- Swimming pools seem like a new invention, but we can thank the Greeks for inventing the first pool in 2500 B.C.E. The Romans invented the first heated pool, and the British later invented the first indoor pools with diving boards!

- Did you know your eyeglasses are magical? Well, not really . . . but the Chinese first invented eyeglasses because they believed colored glasses gave them magical powers. In 1292, Roger Bacon, an English inventor, discovered that magnifying lenses could help people see better.

- What do you call a counting board with grooves in it where pebbles are placed? Discovered in 1899 on the island of Salamis, in Greece, the first real abacus evolved as early as 1200 C.E. in China and was called the *suan-pan*.

- Is there a way you can see inside your own blood cells? Or would you like to see the close-up details of your favorite tiny bug? You can, with the help of the microscope, which was developed by Antonie van Leeuwenhoek in 1674.

- Did Ben Franklin discover electricity? It happened way before that! The German physicist Otto von Guericke experimented with electricity in 1650. English physicist Stephen Gray discovered electrical conductivity in 1729, and Ben Franklin later conducted experiments with his kite during a storm that had lightning!

- In 1792, Eli Whitney finished college and designed the cotton gin in just ten days! This invention takes the seeds from cotton and made the manufacturing of cotton cloth much easier.

- What invention was originally called the "flying chair"? The elevator! King Louis XV of France didn't want to walk around the castle. He complained that there were too many steps from floor to floor! In

1743, his servants created a chair that was controlled by a weight-and-pulley system contained in the chimney! This idea was later improved upon and elevators as we know them today were born!

- Do you know what time it is? Because of Jost Burgi, you do! In 1577, Jost made a "clock" for Tycho Brahe, an astronomer who needed to know the best time to look at the stars. In 1656, the first clock with a pendulum was invented. The pendulum, a long swinging bar at the end of the clock, helped to tell time more accurately.

- In 1759, a Belgian violinist named Joseph Merlin attached wooden spools to his shoes at a costume party and tried to skate around the room. It didn't work, but over 100 years later an American, James Plimpton, created the classic two-by-two-wheel skate design that we know today as roller skates!

- Erno Rubik was a Hungarian teacher who loved math. He invented the Rubik's cube in 1974. He let his students play with it, but they had so much fun with the cube they didn't want to give it back!

RUBIC CUBE MADNESS

- The tradition of throwing disks as a sport started with the ancient Greeks during their Olympics. In the 1940s, students at Yale University tossed around pie tins from the William R. Frisbie bakery. That's why today we call them Frisbees!

- The Slinky was created in 1943 by engineer Richard James of Philadelphia. He was working in his home laboratory when he accidentally knocked one of his springs off a shelf. James saw that the spring "stepped" onto his books to another shelf and then to the floor. James's wife, Betty, said it looked "slinky" and that kids would probably like to watch it "step." The couple sold 500 Slinkys in two hours.

- In 1980, two hockey fans, brothers Scott and Brennan Olson, started their company,

Rollerblade Inc., in their parents' basement! They took an old hockey skate, replaced the sharp blades of the skate with rollers, and added a rubber heel brake!

- The first coin-operated vending machines didn't give out candy, but postcards! They were introduced in England in the 1880s. In 1888, the Adams Gum Company introduced the first vending machines to the United States. The machines were installed on subway platforms in New York City and sold Tutti-Frutti Gum.

- Silly Putty was originally called "nutty putty." It was created by James Wright, who was studying rubber. One day in 1943, Wright accidentally mixed a type of acid with oil, which created a goo that stuck to everything but also copied any newsprint it touched. Did you know that the crew of the space mission *Apollo 8* used Silly Putty to hold down tools in the aircraft while in zero gravity?

- You can thank Edward Binney and Harold Smith every time you take out your Crayola Crayons! These two guys won a gold medal for creating chalk for teachers. Then, in the early 1900s, they created Crayola Crayons out of wax and colored powder. The name Crayola means "oily chalk."

- The idea of "hooping" started when children in ancient Egypt would twirl dried grapevines in the shape of hoops around their waists for fun. Hula hoops were so named because in the early 1800s, British sailors visited the Hawaiian Islands and noted the similarity between "hooping" and hula dancing. It wasn't until the 1950s that hula hoops became popular and were sold in stores.

- Everyone knows the Etch A Sketch! At first, nobody wanted to buy the invention that Arthur Granjean created in his garage. It wasn't until Arthur starting running TV commercials for the Etch A Sketch that everyone wanted their very own. Arthur Granjean wanted everyone to be able to create art, anywhere, at any time!

- The yo-yo has been around for over 2,500 years, since the time of the ancient Greeks! It wasn't until the 1900s, however, that the toy received the name yo-yo.

Pedro Flores, a young man in the Philippines, noticed that whenever he played with the wooden toy people would crowd around and watch him. He called his toy a yo-yo, which means "come-come" in Tagalog, the native language of the Philippines.

- Mr. Potato Head was born in 1952 in Rhode Island — but not in a potato field! When Mr. Potato Head was first dreamed up, you had to supply your own potato, and then you were given plastic eyes, nose, ears, and mouth. It wasn't until years later that the plastic body was invented.

POTATO HEAD EVOLUTION

- What was the first video game ever invented? If you guessed Pong — as in Ping-Pong — you're right. Pong was invented in 1958 by Wily Higinbotham. Working at a nuclear research company, Higinbotham created this game to show people the possible paths of nuclear missiles.

- Ole Kirk Christensen was a carpenter who made wooden toys. In 1932, he bought a plastic mold-making machine and soon after he began making LEGOs in his basement. The word LEGOs means "play well together" in Danish.

- Did you know that Barbie is a real person? Well, she was *modeled* after one, anyway! In the 1950s, a woman named Ruth Handler noticed that her daughter Barbara loved playing with dolls. She created the Barbie doll and named it after her daughter. She sold the Barbie doll idea to Mattel, and they have sold more than a billion dolls!

- Everybody owns a pair of blue jeans! But did you know that Levi Strauss got the idea from a friend of his who was a tailor? Together, they created the first pair of blue jeans in 1873.

- The skateboard was originally invented in the 1960s by California surfers who were mad when it was too rainy to surf. They started to nail the wheels from roller skates to the front and back ends of wooden planks. The boards allowed for "sidewalk surfing" along streets.

- Do you like PEZ candy? Do you know where the name came from? It comes from the German word for peppermint! The original PEZ was created in 1927 in a peppermint flavor only. It was sold as a breath mint and there was no fun toy head at the top. It wasn't until 1952 that the fruity flavor and toy part were added!

- Dr. John S. Pemberton invented the Coca-Cola recipe in 1885, but at first nobody would purchase his sweet drink. In 1892, he decided to add carbonation — bubbles — to the original recipe and then everyone started to buy it.

- George Washington Carver invented peanut butter along with more than three hundred other uses for peanuts and even more uses for pecans and sweet potatoes. He helped invent many other things, too, including adhesives, bleach, buttermilk, chili sauce, instant coffee, paper, plastic, shaving cream, shoe polish, talcum powder, and wood stain.

- Believe it or not, tea was discovered in 2737 B.C.E. by a great Chinese emperor named Shen Nung. He was boiling water when leaves from a nearby bush fell into the kettle. Shen Nung smelled the mixture and tea was invented!

THOSE DIRTY LEAVES SMELL GOOD ENOUGH TO DRINK!

- The year was 1904, and Charles Menches was selling ice cream at a fair and ran out of dishes. Nearby, his friend Ernest Hamwi, who was from Syria, was selling a treat called *zalabia*. Zalabia is a crisp, waferlike pastry sold with syrup. Menches rolled up the zalabia, scooped his ice cream on top, and the ice-cream cone was born!

- Potato chips were invented by Chef George Crum in New England in 1853 when a customer sent back his french fries. The customer said the potatoes were too thick. So, just to make that customer mad, Chef Crum made the potatoes so thin that they could not be eaten with a fork!

- A Fig Newton, if you don't already know, is a soft cookie filled with fig jam. A machine invented in 1891 made Fig Newtons possible. James Henry Mitchell invented a machine where the inside funnel supplied jam, while the outside funnel pumped out the dough.

- Have we always eaten with knives, forks, and spoons? Well, at first people used their hands, then shells to scoop up food, then they used bread, and then finally, the Greeks started using utensils in the seventh century C.E.

- What do you call popcorn, peanuts, and molasses? Cracker Jack! In 1896, Louis Rueckheim discovered how to keep the molasses-covered popcorn morsels from sticking together. This formula is still a BIG secret.

- Do you like 7 Up? Did you know it was first called Whistle and then Howdy before it was finally called 7 Up? Orange Crush and 7 Up were both invented in 1919. Orange Crush was the most popular orange soft drink after it was invented.

- Do you like hot dogs? In the 1920s, German sausage or "wieners" were very popular. Harry Magely, a caterer in New York, told the vendors to sell them by shouting, "Get your red hots!" Magely and Charles Feltman, who was from Coney Island, are both responsible for coming up with the idea of the bun.

- Did you know that Jell-O didn't always taste like it does now? At first it was just plain gelatin, which is made from animal bones. It wasn't until Mr. P. B. Wait, who made cough syrup, decided to add fruit syrup that it got its sweet flavor. By the early 1900s everyone was eating Jell-O.

- Walter Diemer was an accountant who worked at a gum factory. He was bored with his job, and in 1928 he decided to try to make a kind of gum that would make bubbles. He worked in his basement and made hundreds of recipes until he created the first bubble gum. He took his first five-pound bag to a general store and it sold out in one hour!

- Amedeo Obici, the founder of Planters Peanuts, was born in 1876 near Venice, Italy. He came to the United States when he was only 11 years old, but he was very willing to work. From a horse and a wagon, he began to sell fruits and peanuts, calling himself The Peanut Specialist. The Mr. Peanut drawing was based on Amedeo himself.

- In 1905, Frank Epperson invented the Popsicle stick, or as he called it, the Eppesicle! He was 11 years old when he accidentally left his drink outside on the picnic table. That night, the temperature dropped, and when Frank came out the next morning, the straw had frozen in his drink. Frank showed his friends at school, but he didn't start adding fruit flavors and making his Eppesicles until 20 years later!

- In 1930, Ruth and Ken Wakefield bought an old-style "toll house" near Boston, which they eventually called the Toll House Inn, a restaurant. Ruth loved to make desserts and one afternoon while baking, she put Nestlé semisweet chocolate chips in her sugar cookies and invented the Nestlé Toll House cookie!

- Peppermint Life Savers were invented by a man who made chocolates. Nobody would buy Clarence Crane's chocolates in the summer because they melted. So, in 1912, he created Crane's Peppermint Life Savers so he could also earn money in the summertime.

- In 1912, Jim Kirby got so tired of seeing his mom work at cleaning that he invented a nonelectric vacuum. Later, in the 1930s, George Scott and Carl Fetzer thought Jim had great ideas and hired him to create all different kinds of electric vacuums.

- Canned food was invented in 1813 for the British navy. They had to use hammers to smash open their cans! The can opener wasn't invented until 50 years later.

- Do you use Ivory soap? Did you ever notice that it floats? It is the only soap that floats, and it happened by accident. In the 1800s, an employee failed to shut off the soap-making machine when he went to lunch. When he returned, he found the soap mixture puffed-up and frothy. The extra air made the soap lighter than water. The company later received letters telling them that their soap floated!

- Thanks to Paul Nipkow, you can watch your favorite cartoons on TV! Television was based on an 1884 device called the scanning disk, which was invented by 14-year-old Paul Nipkow. In 1939, an American company bought Paul's ideas, which eventually led to the creation of the television you watch today!

- The first TV remote control was called Lazy Bones, because you didn't have to get up to change the channel. It was developed in 1950 by Zenith.

- Spencer Silver was a scientist who worked for a glue company called 3M. In 1970, Spencer created a glue that wasn't very strong, but his friend Arthur Fry decided he could still find a use for it. Arthur sang in a choir and always marked the pages in his songbooks with slips of paper, which often fell out. Using Silver's weak glue, he made the perfect thing to keep his markers in place without damaging the book — Post-it Notes!

PRANKSTERS AT THE POST-IT NOTE COMPANY

- Catharine Beecher came up with the idea of soaking and scrubbing clothes against a washboard in water to get the dirt out. That was the very first washing machine, invented in 1797! The first *electric* washer was introduced in the U.S. in 1908.

- Do you ever wonder how the clothes we wear are made? Sewing machines weren't invented until 1851, but the idea began back in 1755 when an American inventor named Charles T. Wiesenthal invented the double-pointed needle — something that's in every sewing machine today!

- Can you name a kitchen appliance that is very cool and makes you feel better when you're hungry? That's right . . . the refrigerator! This awesome invention took three people and 39 years to finally get it right in 1855!

- Imagine if every time you had a tummy ache or headache, your mom would make you bite down on the bark of a willow tree! Well, ever since the ancient Greeks, people have used willow bark to relieve pain. In 1853, a French scientist named Charles Gergardt made a pill that used willow bark. It wasn't until 1899 that German sci-

TUMMY ACHE, DADDY?

entist Felix Hoffman, who was looking for a remedy for his dad's arthritis, perfected the pill that we know today as aspirin.

- George de Mestral, a Swiss engineer, returned from a walk one day in 1948 and found there were burrs from a bush stuck to his jacket. Realizing that the burr stuck because of its tiny natural hooks, he went on to invent hook-and-loop fastener — otherwise known as Velcro®!

BIRTH OF A MILLION-DOLLAR IDEA

- When matches were first invented, they were very large and bulky. In 1889, Joshua Pusey, a lawyer from Pennsylvania, was on his way to a dinner party. He smoked cigars and wanted to bring his matches, but the huge box of wooden matches looked ridiculous sticking out of his vest! So, later he invented paper matches, and everyone started to buy them!

- In 1893, Witcom Judson invented a "hookless fastener," but it still wasn't easy to put on your clothes! In 1913, Gideon Sundback, a Swedish scientist who was working in the United States, invented an easier fastener: the zipper!

- DVDs are discs that store information like CDs. What makes them different is that they can hold a lot more information than CDs, for such things as movies. One person did not create DVD technology. It took many companies and their employees to make DVD a reality in 1995.

- In the winter of 1948, Kay Draper of Michigan discovered a big problem. The sandpile that she normally used for her cat's litter box was totally frozen. She then tried using ashes in the litter box, but that left paw prints all over her house! One day she ran into a next-door neighbor who suggested using clay pellets . . . and Kitty Litter was born!

- Stephen J. Poplawski invented the blender in 1922. Poplawski was the first to put a spinning blade at the bottom of a container to make shakes. In 1935, Fred Waring, along with inventor Frederick Osius, improved on the idea and made the kitchen blender!

- Hungarian journalist Ladislas Biro and his brother, Georg, invented the first ballpoint pen. Unfortunately, World War II stopped production of their invention. But the American company Eberhard Faber paid the Biro brothers $500,000 for the rights to make the pens. In 1945, Gimble's department store sold 10,000 pens in one afternoon!

- A French scientist named Nicolas Conte developed pencils in 1795. He used a mixture of clay and graphite that was fired before it was put into a wooden case.

- Albert J. Parkhouse worked at the Timberlake Wire Company in 1903. He went to hang up his coat at work and found all the hooks were taken. He picked up a piece of wire on the floor, bent it, and hung up his coat. Unfortunately, his company took credit for the invention of the clothes hanger, and they made all the money from his idea!

- Bette Nesmith Graham was a secretary and an artist. She was working with paints one day in 1956 when she used her blender to make the very first bottle of Liquid Paper. She needed the correctional fluid to cover up the mistakes she made on her papers at work!

- Sarah Boone needed a device that would help straighten out the wrinkles in clothing. She invented the ironing board in 1892.

- Percy Spencer was an electronics genius! One day in 1946, while touring one of the laboratories at his company, he stopped in front of a magnetron machine and noticed that the chocolate bar in his pocket began to melt. He then went out and bought some unpopped popcorn. Holding the bag of corn next to the magnetron, Spencer watched as the kernels exploded into puffy white morsels. The microwave oven was born!

- For his wife, inventor John W. Hammes built the world's first kitchen garbage disposal unit in 1927. He went into business selling his invention and named his company the In-Sink-Erator Manufacturing Company.

- Walter H. Deubner owned a store and wanted to make more money. He figured that if the customers could carry more, they would buy more. He designed a package that was made of paper with a cord running through it. Deubner was selling a million paper bags a year by 1915!

- One of the very first computers ever built weighed seven hundred pounds, had over three hundred vacuum tubes, and over a mile of wire! Built by Professor John Atanasoff and his student John Berry in 1939, this computer was very slow. It could do one operation in fifteen seconds, whereas today's computers can do 150 billion operations every fifteen seconds!

- We save our coins in piggy banks because someone made a mistake! During the Middle Ages, pots were made of clay called pygg. People put their extra coins in a clay pot. They called this their pygg bank. In the 19th century, when English potters received requests for piggy banks, they produced banks shaped like pigs.

- Who was Earl Tupper? Do you know what Tupperware is? In 1942, Tupper began to make a bathroom drinking glass available in a rainbow of colors and quickly moved on to his famous plastic food storage boxes!

• Arthur Scott owned a paper products company in the 1900s. One day, a railroad car full of paper that had been rolled too thick for toilet paper came to the plant. He had heard of a teacher who would give a small piece of soft paper to students with runny noses so the roller towel in the rest rooms would not become contaminated with germs. Scott realized that his thick paper could be used after all — as paper towels!

• Marion Donovan was a mom who was tired of leaky cloth diapers that had to be washed. In 1950, she invented a plastic covering for cloth diapers from a shower curtain. She combined the plastic with a super-absorbent material and a year later the disposable diaper was born.

• The idea for fax machines has been around since 1842, when Alexander Bain invented a machine capable of receiving signals from a telegraph wire and translating them into images on paper. In 1850, a London inventor named F. C. Blakewell created a similar machine, which he called a copying telegraph. It wasn't until 1966 that the Xerox company began distributing a small machine similar to the fax machines of today.

• Say "cheese" for Niepce, the inventor of the first camera! In 1816, he set up a camera in the window of his home, left it there for most of the day, and wound up with a grainy, blurry photograph of the

rooftops nearby. He was the first person to record an image permanently as a photograph!

- Ever clean your ears with a Q-tip? Well, these tiny cotton swabs were invented by Leo Gerstenzang in the 1920s. Leo's wife wanted something to clean their baby's ears after bathtime. She began using a toothpick stuck into a piece of cotton. Leo spent years improving upon that idea!

- The first sneakers were invented in the mid-1800s and were called plimsolls. In 1917, rubber-soled shoes were first sold as sneakers by United States Rubber and were called Keds. In 1972, Nike Inc. began using waffle soles, made by pressing rubber into a waffle iron!

- The World Wide Web was developed in 1989 by English computer scientist Timothy Berners-Lee. Now you can buy your favorite toys, books, food — all without leaving your house!

- Do you like books or comic strips? Without the printing press they wouldn't exist! Movable type for a printing press was invented by Johannes Gutenberg in 1450. Once developed, everyone used the printing press, and it began to replace handwritten papers.

- The dictionaries in your classroom were first developed in the 1880s! Way before you were born, the people at Merriam-Webster started files of all the words people use. Dictionaries contain nearly 15 million examples of words used all over the world.

- In the early 1900s, women dried their hair by using vacuum cleaners! The vacuum blew air out in those days! The first real hand-held hair dryer was invented in 1951.

- Conrad Hubert, a Russian immigrant, had a friend named Joshua Lionel Cowen who invented a flowerpot with a battery in it. The battery made the flowerpot light up.

Hubert took the battery, the lightbulb, and the paper tube from the pot and remade it into what he called "an electric hand torch." This is what we call a flashlight!

- The Fardier was a three-wheeled, steam-powered vehicle built in 1771 by Nicolas Joseph Cugnot. This was never put on the road because it was so slow!

- Orville and Wilbur Wright were American inventors who started out fixing bicycles. In 1899, they built their first flying machine, which was a biplane kite that they had fitted with wings. They completed their first powered airplane and made history's first powered and controlled airplane flight in 1903.

- Henry Ford sold over 18 million cars by 1927 and invented the idea of the assembly line, where each person is responsible for doing one specific job over and over again. He built a gasoline-powered car in 1896.

- In 1903, Mary Anderson saw drivers roll down their car windows when it rained in order to see the road. She decided to do something about it and invented windshield wipers, which we see on every car today!

- The steam-powered locomotive, or train, was invented by Richard Trevithick and Oliver Evans in 1803. A steam engine is an engine that uses heated water to generate power. But did you know that the earliest steam engines were used by the ancient Greeks in the first century C.E.?

- When it was first invented in 1791, the first bicycle looked more like a scooter. Called *draisines* after the German man who invented them, these first bikes were not very fast at all. It wasn't until 1839 that a man named Kirkpatrick MacMillan added pedals and brakes to make the bicycle move faster — and to slow it down!

- The first space shuttle was launched by NASA in 1981. *Columbia* was the name of the shuttle, and it was the first spacecraft designed to be reusable.

- Ever wonder where the snowmobile came from? Well, in 1927, Carl J. Eliason came up with the idea for a motorized toboggan. But snowmobiles are not just for fun. Many snowmobiles are driven by police, workers servicing telephone lines, ranchers and farmers, trappers, and rescue-squad crews.

- In 1973, the General Motors research team invented the first safety air bags for cars — but nobody wanted them! In 1986, air bags were offered again as an option on the Ford Tempo. Chrysler became the first company to offer air bag systems as standard equipment in 1988.

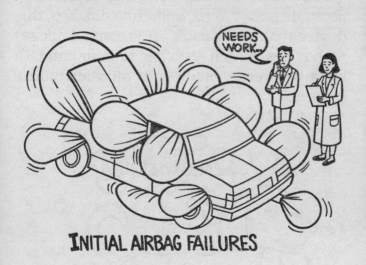

INITIAL AIRBAG FAILURES

Each of the following are real *inventions thought up by* real *people! These are just a few of the many inventions that people have thought of but have never been used.*

• Did you ever think your dog could use a portable potty? Well, someone did. Yep, this device that never took off is a small bucket with ropes, which attaches to your animal's back to prevent accidents on your mom's carpet!

• When you go to the beach, do you ever notice that your feet are the only part of your body that never gets tan? Well, if you used the Foot Elevator, they would! This invention is a set of plastic feet (sort of like the steel shoe slide that measures your foot in a shoe store) with sticks that sit in the sand and elevate your feet to be closer to the sun.

• Do you have a younger brother or sister in diapers? Wouldn't you like to be able to tell whether or not his or her diaper is dirty? Then you would need the Diaper Alarm. What you would do is place your brother or sister on this metal block and, with a small jolt of electricity, it would be able to tell if the baby's diaper is full. Can you guess why this invention never made it?

• The Bat Boy was designed to help kids get better use from their in-line skates. A set of mechanical wings was meant to help you gain speed when you're learning to skate. This invention never got off the ground because there was too much equipment for kids to carry around.

• Floating Furniture might be something that your parents would use to save space in your house. The furniture would be similar to the floats you use in the pool, except that these would be filled with helium so they would stay on the ceiling all day — until you pulled the ropes to bring them down to the floor!

• Now, here's an invention that hasn't taken off just yet, but it's not a bad idea. How would you feel if your ice-cream cone could spin around so that all you had to do was stick out your tongue?

ACME
CONE SPINNER

• There is nothing worse than stinky feet. So someone invented a mini-air-conditioning system for your stinky sneakers. Actually, it is only a pair of sneakers with holes in them. So hold on to those old sneakers and start poking holes!

• Somewhere between a Boogie board and a Jet Ski is the invention of the Jet-Powered Surfboard. We haven't seen any out there in great numbers, but it may be the best way to ride waves in the future.

• Imagine if your toilet was lit up like a Christmas tree. Or like an airplane runway! Someone has actually invented toilet landing lights. While they are not in the stores yet, they could be the next thing on your little brother's Christmas list.

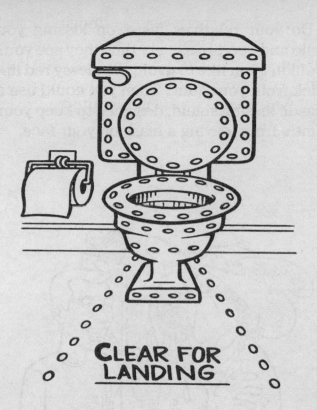

CLEAR FOR LANDING

• When was the last time you got stuck washing the family dog? What if he could wash himself? This device is a bucket of soapy water attached to your dog's stomach. It is attached to a sprinkler on the dog's collar that leaves your dog squeaky clean.

• Do your relatives insist on kissing you hello and good-bye every time they see you? Wouldn't you like to avoid the messy red lipstick from your aunt? Then you could use a plastic kissing shield, designed to keep your auntie from leaving a mark on your face.

Dorothea DePrisco worked in publishing for seven years before moving to the island of Lana'i, in Hawaii. She taught high school English at Lana'i High and Elementary in Lana'i City. She is currently living in Los Angeles with her cats, Felix and Lucy, and works as a freelance writer.